18 Thinking about how to behave
The Buddha taught his followers how to behave in a way that is fair for all beings.

20 Worshipping the Buddha
Buddhists worship the Buddha to show respect and thanks for his life and teaching.

22 Buddhism - a joyful religion
There are four things that bring happiness in life: love, compassion, joy and being peaceful.

24 Celebrating a commitment
A Buddhist marriage is a commitment between the bride and groom to live by the Buddha's teachings.

26 Death, rebirth and Nibbana
Buddhism teaches that we live through many lives on Earth. The way we behave in one life affects us in the next life.

28 Celebrating the end of a life
A Buddhist funeral is a time to celebrate the life of someone who has died.

30 Glossary and more information
An explanation of the bold words in the book and ideas on where to find out more about Buddhism.

32 Index
Use this to find topics in the book that interest you.

12 Learning about Buddhism

20 Worshipping the Buddha

24 A Buddhist wedding ceremony in Cambodia

How to use this book

People who follow Buddhism are known as **Buddhists**. This book tells you what it is like to be a Buddhist and about the special times, customs and beliefs of Buddhists.

Finding your way

The pages in this book have been carefully planned to make it easy for you to find out about Buddhism. Here are two examples with explanations about the different features. Look at the Contents pages too, to read about each section.

---

20   Way of life

Worshipping the Buddha

Buddhists do not believe that the Buddha is a god. They worship him to show respect and thanks for his life and teachings. There are no rules about how often Buddhists should worship, or when.

These prayer wheels contain blessings written on paper. Some Buddhists spin prayer wheels and imagine the blessings spreading all over the world.

At the temple

Buddhists may worship in a temple or at home. Those who live near a temple may worship there regularly in the **shrine** hall. They may also gather there with friends for Buddhist festivals. The style of worship varies from country to country, but may include chanting verses from scriptures, lighting **incense** and candles, offering fresh flowers or fruit and bowing to the Buddha-figure on the shrine.

People sit or kneel for worship. They may chant verses to commit themselves to relying on the Buddha's example, his teachings and the community of Buddhists. They may chant in the ancient Indian languages of Pali or Sanskrit, or in their own languages.

Usually worship is led by a monk, but in some **traditions** it may be led by a nun or other Buddhists.

Jane is 8 years old. She lives in Scotland, UK.

We don't live near a temple so my family worships at home. We take it in turns to light a candle and my mum picks special flowers from our garden to put in front of the Buddha. Then we chant and meditate. Meditating is my favourite part because it gives me time to think. Twice a year we go to the temple in the city. I really like going because I get to meet other Buddhist children.

Case studies give a Buddhist person's own experience of a custom described in the section.

Captions give a short description of a picture.

A journey through life in

Buddhism

Contents

Published by A & C Black Publishers
Limited
36 Soho Square
London W1D 3QY
www.acblack.com

ISBN 978-1-4081-2965-4

Copyright © A & C Black Publishers
Limited 2010

Series concept: Suma Din
Series consultant: Lynne Broadbent
Buddhist consultant: Munisha, Education
Officer, The Clear Vision Trust

Created by Bookwork Ltd, Stroud, UK

A CIP catalogue record for this book is
available from the British Library.

A & C Black uses paper produced with
elemental chlorine-free pulp, harvested
from managed sustainable forests. It
is natural, renewable and recyclable.
The logging and manufacturing process
conform to the environmental regulations
of the country of origin.

Printed in China by Leo Paper Products

4 How to use this book
An explanation of all the different features you will find in this book.

6 Welcoming a new baby
Many Buddhist families have a naming ceremony for their baby.

8 The Buddha's Enlightenment
When the Buddha reached Enlightenment, he understood the Way Life Really Is. Buddhists celebrate his Enlightenment in the festival of Wesak.

10 The Buddhist community
Living in a Buddhist community is like living with good friends who help each other. Friendship and community are important to Buddhists.

12 The teachings of the Buddha
The Buddha taught people about the Way Life Really Is. His teachings tell us how to end suffering and reach Enlightenment.

14 The importance of kindness
Buddhism teaches the importance of doing our best to be kind to all living things. The more kindly we behave, the kinder we become. Kindness leads to true happiness.

16 How our actions affect others
Buddhists believe that everything we do affects other living things. Kind actions lead to happiness. Unkind actions cause suffering.

Comments give additional information about something specific in a picture.

Buddhist girls worshipping at a temple in Cambodia. There are Buddhists in most countries of the world.

The girls are kneeling with their hands together to show their respect for the Buddha.

Over to you... asks the reader to think more about their own customs and beliefs and how they compare to Buddhist beliefs.

Quotes are taken from the Buddha's teachings.

Over to y...

● Who or what admire most? Ho you show this?

● Do you have favourite time of

Buddhism — a joyful religion

Buddhism is a joyful **faith**. Buddhists believe that the kinder and more generous we try to be, the more joy we will have in our lives. Happiness is a good habit we can learn.

The Laughing Buddha
The Laughing Buddha was born 1,000 years ago in China. He was a Buddhist monk and teacher. He gained Enlightenment so he was known as a Buddha. He is admired for his kindness, generosity, **wisdom** and contentment.

A statue of the Laughing Buddha in China.

If we maintain a sense of joy, not only will we experience inner happiness and peace, but the fruits of our practice will swiftly arise.

Over to you...
● What sort of things bring joy into your life? What do you do to bring joy into your life and other people's lives?

Many Buddhas
Buddha is a title for anyone who is Enlightened. Siddattha became the first Buddha, and other people have become Buddhas since. Some Buddhists worship symbolic, imaginary Buddhas. The statues of symbolic Buddhas shown here are in Japan and Singapore.

Bringing joy into everyday life
The Buddha taught that there were four things that would bring about happiness in life: love, compassion, joy and equanimity.

● Love means wanting others to be happy.
● Compassion means showing love for people who are suffering.
● Joy means being happy at someone else's good fortune and not being jealous.
● Equanimity means keeping a calm and peaceful mind, no matter what happens.

Bold words in the text are explained more fully in the glossary on page 30.

Boxed text gives extra information about a subject on the page.

Welcoming a new baby

The birth of a baby is a special day in every family. Around the world, Buddhists have different **rituals** to welcome a new baby. Many give their babies a naming ceremony.

Two families celebrate the naming of their babies at a Buddhist temple in the UK.

Naming ceremony

At the naming ceremony, a monk passes a piece of white thread around the room so that everyone is holding it. One end is tied to the hand of a **Buddha** figure and the other to the baby's wrist. Some Buddhists use red thread because that's the colour of blood, and blood flows through everyone – like life. The thread is a way of showing that the baby has been welcomed as part of their **community**.

The monk chants some special words of blessing from the Buddhist **scriptures**. Then the thread is cut. Everyone ties a piece around the wrist of the person next to them. This is so everyone remembers that they are part of the same community as the family. Afterwards there may be a party.

What's in a name?

Traditional Buddhist names have a meaning. For example, Jaya means 'victory' and Pema means 'lotus' (a kind of flower). If Buddhists choose a Buddhist name for their baby, they hope it will help their child to live kindly and wisely.

Jyoti is 6 years old. She lives in the UK and had a naming ceremony soon after she was born.

I was born in Cheshire in the UK. My mum and dad are Buddhists, so they decided to give me a naming ceremony a few months after my birth. They gave me a traditional Buddhist name. Jyoti means 'light' or 'the shining one'. I really like my name and it makes me want to live up to it.

Over to you...

● Imagine you are a Buddhist. How might you feel, taking home a bit of the thread?

● Have you been to a naming ceremony? How soon did this happen after the baby's birth?

This Chinese baby's name is Kuanyin. This is the name of the Buddha of compassion.

The Buddha's Enlightenment

The word 'Buddha' is a title. It means 'Awakened one' or 'one who has reached **Enlightenment**' – a perfectly kind and wise person. The Buddha said anyone could become a Buddha.

The Buddha is shown with a halo (a ring of light) around his head. It shows he is sacred to Buddhists.

The Buddha

The Buddha was born 2,500 years ago. His parents gave him the name Siddattha, which means 'One who will achieve his goals'. He was born into a rich family and did not know that suffering and death existed in the world.

When Siddattha realised that everyone is unhappy sometimes, he had lots of questions. Why do people suffer? How can we be happy? For years, he calmed his mind and body through **meditation**.

One night in May, Siddattha was meditating when he realised that he had the answers to his questions. He understood the Way Life Really Is. He spent the rest of his long life teaching other people the way to happiness.

Meditation is very important to many Buddhists. It is a way of training the heart and mind. The Buddha said:

"All that we are is the result of what we have thought. The mind is everything. What we think we become."

Over to you...

● Do you ever sit quietly to think and relax? Where do you go to do this?

● What do you do to help you to feel calm?

Celebrating Wesak

Buddhists celebrate the Enlightenment of the Buddha during the festival of **Wesak** in May. Many celebrate his birthday at the same time. They go to the temple and listen to stories about the Buddha and the wise things he said. They light candles and meditate. Then there is a feast with friends.

For many Buddhists, Wesak is the most important festival of the year. In some countries, such as Sri Lanka, Thailand and Vietnam, Wesak is a national holiday.

Newari women celebrate Wesak in Nepal. They are holding a white thread to show they are connected in a community.

The Buddhist community

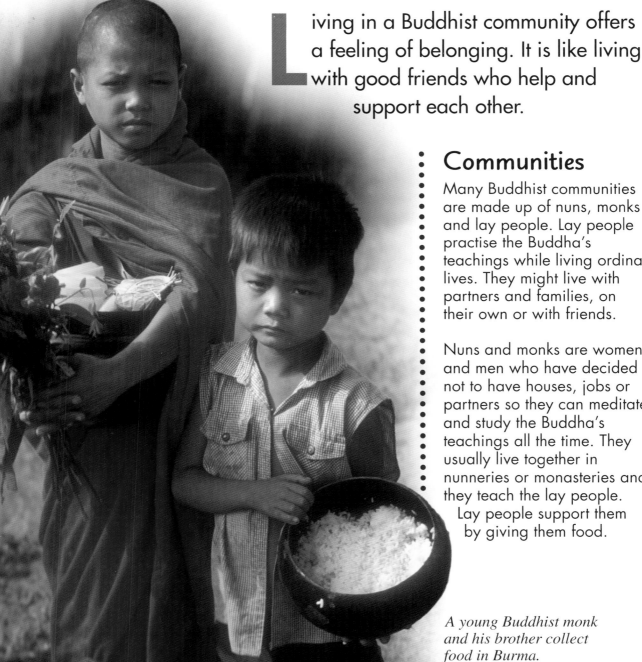

Living in a Buddhist community offers a feeling of belonging. It is like living with good friends who help and support each other.

Communities

Many Buddhist communities are made up of nuns, monks and lay people. Lay people practise the Buddha's teachings while living ordinary lives. They might live with partners and families, on their own or with friends.

Nuns and monks are women and men who have decided not to have houses, jobs or partners so they can meditate and study the Buddha's teachings all the time. They usually live together in nunneries or monasteries and they teach the lay people. Lay people support them by giving them food.

A young Buddhist monk and his brother collect food in Burma.

Young Buddhists

In some countries, many young boys become **novices** and go to monasteries to study. They learn the words of the Buddha and practise meditation. They follow the **vinaya** – the rules or way of life of the monastery. The novices also have to do housework and chores. When they are older, some novices choose to become monks. Others choose to go back to their families.

Friendship and community are very important to Buddhists. The Buddha said:

"Friendship is the only cure for hatred, the only guarantee of peace."

Young monks in Burma study the wise words of the Buddha.

A Buddhist community in the UK gather in a temple for a festival when they give gifts, such as food, to the monks.

Buddhist monks wear different coloured robes to show they are living a special life.

The teachings of the Buddha

Buddhists do not believe in a god who made all things. They see the Buddha as a leader who taught people about the Way Life Really Is.

Central beliefs

The Buddha's most important teachings are known as the **Dhamma**. They include:

- The Four Noble Truths
- The Eightfold Path
- The importance of kindness
- That everything we do affects others

This wall painting shows the Buddha teaching monks and animals in the countryside.

The Four Noble Truths

The Four Noble Truths explain about human suffering and tell us how to end suffering.

- Everyone experiences suffering in life.
- We suffer because we want things that cannot make us happy for long – some new shoes, for example.
- It is possible to stop relying on these less helpful things over time.
- The way to do this is to follow the Eightfold Path, which leads to happiness.

Each of the spokes in the Wheel of Dhamma represents one part of the Eightfold Path.

Right View (understanding)

Right Meditation (concentration)

Right Thought

Right Mindfulness (awareness)

Right Speech

Right Effort

Right Action

Right Livelihood

The Eightfold Path

The Eightfold Path lists eight things that Buddhists can do to end suffering and reach Enlightenment. Buddhists are reminded of these things by the Dhammachakka, or the Wheel of Dhamma, which has eight spokes.

Being kind

Buddhists believe that actions speak louder than words. The Buddha said:

However many holy words you hear, however many you speak, what good will they do if you do not act upon them?

This Wheel of Dhamma is on the roof of a monastery in Lhasa, Tibet.

The importance of kindness

Kindness can make you happy. Have you ever done something for someone else and felt good about it? This is what Buddhists mean when they say kindness is its own reward.

The path to true happiness

Buddhists believe that the more kindly a person behaves, the kinder they become. One day they will behave with kindness and **generosity** all the time, without thinking about it. This is the behaviour of a Buddha.

The Buddha taught people to train themselves to become peaceful, wise and kind to all living things. He taught that true happiness comes from kindness and contentment. Of course, it's not enough just to wish for these things, we must work for them through our actions.

The Buddha taught that everything relies on other things. Everything is changing, but we can develop stillness and peace from following his teachings.

A woman in a Burmese village gives some rice to Buddhist monks.

The monks rely on the kindness of villagers.

Over to you...

● Can you think of any times when you've been kind to someone and it's made you happy?

● How do you know when you've done something good? Is it because someone tells you it is good? Is it because it feels good? Or is it something else?

The 14th Dalai Lama leads prayers at a public gathering.

A Buddhist leader

Buddhists around the world have many different beliefs and leaders. The Dalai Lama is the spiritual and political leader of many Tibetan Buddhists. Followers of the Dalai Lama believe that when he dies, he is reborn in a new human life. This is called **rebirth**. A search party sets out to find the boy who will be the new Dalai Lama. The searchers look for clues that will show them who to look for and where he is.

There is no need for temples; no need for complicated **philosophy.** *Our own brain, our own heart is our temple; the philosophy is kindness.*

How our actions affect others

The Buddha taught that we are all connected. Buddhists believe that the way we behave affects people around us and that all actions have consequences (results). This is the teaching of **kamma**.

The tick on this cup of tea shows that the tea was fairly traded. This means that the poor farmers who grew the tea were paid a fair price for it.

Kamma

The word 'kamma' means 'action'. The Buddha taught that kind, generous, thoughtful actions lead to happiness for us and for others. Selfish, unkind and thoughtless actions cause suffering. Even a thoughtful choice about what food and drink we buy in the supermarket can affect many lives.

Druki is 10 years old and lives in the UK. She is talking to her aunt.

"Would you like a cup of tea?" asked Aunty Charini.

"Yes please," I said.

"Do you know where tea comes from?" asked Aunty Charini.

"From the supermarket," I said.

Aunty Charini laughed. "The tea you're drinking was grown in Africa. The young leaves are picked during the growing season. Lots of women work as tea pickers. They carry baskets on their backs and put the leaves inside. Then they take them to the factory where they are dried and crushed. Finally, the tea is sent by ship to Britain where it is packaged into foil and boxes. Then it is sent from the supermarket's distribution centre to our town — and that's where I bought it. That's a lot of people to make one cup of tea."

"It's a lovely cup of tea," I said.

"Yes it is," said Aunty Charini.

This man shaves his head and wears a simple robe to show he is a monk.

Schoolchildren visit a monastery in the UK to learn about Buddhism.

Over to you...

● Think about the food you ate today. How far had it travelled to get to your plate? Who grew it? Who prepared it and cooked it?

Thinking about how to behave

There are no commandments, or rules, in Buddhism. Instead, the Buddha suggested what people should do to bring happiness to themselves and other people.

The Five Ethical Precepts

The Buddha taught his followers to act, think and speak kindly. He gave them Five Ethical Precepts – guidelines on how to behave in a way that is right and fair for all beings.

- Avoid harming living beings; practise loving kindness instead.
- Avoid taking things that don't belong to you; be generous instead.
- Avoid selfishness in **relationships**; be content whether you are single or have a partner.
- Avoid lies and telling tales; speak truthfully and kindly.
- Avoid alcohol and drugs that cloud the mind; keep a clear head.

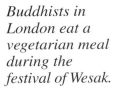

Buddhists in London eat a vegetarian meal during the festival of Wesak.

Choosing what food to eat

Some Buddhists choose not to eat meat or fish because they don't want to harm animals. This is easy if there is plenty of food. If there is not much food, a person might need to eat meat and fish to stay healthy. Humans are also living things who need care.

Many Buddhists think carefully about the environment and pollution when they choose what to eat. They might think about food miles (how far food has travelled from where it was grown to the shop), and whether a lot of fuel was used to get it to the shop.

They also consider whether food has been grown by someone in a very poor country who doesn't earn much money, and whether it was fairly traded (whether that person was paid a fair price).

This basket of lotus flower buds and food is a temple offering to the Buddha.

" *Today may we appreciate this food and remember those who are hungry.* "

Worshipping the Buddha

Buddhists do not believe that the Buddha is a god. They worship him to show respect and thanks for his life and teachings. There are no rules about how often Buddhists should worship, or when.

These prayer wheels contain blessings written on paper. Some Buddhists spin prayer wheels and imagine the blessings spreading all over the world.

At the temple

Buddhists may worship in a temple or at home. Those who live near a temple may worship there regularly in the **shrine** hall. They may also gather there with friends for Buddhist festivals. The style of worship varies from country to country, but may include chanting verses from scriptures, lighting **incense** and candles, offering fresh flowers or fruit and bowing to the Buddha-figure on the shrine.

People sit or kneel for worship. They may chant verses to commit themselves to relying on the Buddha's example, his teachings and the community of Buddhists. They may chant in the ancient Indian languages of Pali or Sanskrit, or in their own languages.

Usually worship is led by a monk, but in some **traditions** it may be led by a nun or other Buddhists.

We don't live near a temple so my family worships at home. We take it in turns to light a candle and my mum picks special flowers from our garden to put in front of the Buddha. Then we chant and meditate. Meditating is my favourite part because it gives me time to think. Twice a year we go to the temple in the city. I really like going because I get to meet other Buddhist children.

Jane is 8 years old. She lives in Scotland, UK.

Buddhist girls worshipping at a temple in Cambodia. There are Buddhists in most countries of the world.

The girls are kneeling with their hands together to show their respect for the Buddha.

Over to you...

● Who or what do you admire most? How do you show this?

● Do you have a favourite time of day?

Buddhism — a joyful religion

Buddhism is a joyful **faith**. Buddhists believe that the kinder and more generous we try to be, the more joy we will have in our lives. Happiness is a good habit we can learn.

The Laughing Buddha

The Laughing Buddha was born 1,000 years ago in China. He was a Buddhist monk and teacher. He gained Enlightenment so he was known as a Buddha. He is admired for his kindness, generosity, **wisdom** and contentment.

A statue of the Laughing Buddha in China.

If we maintain a sense of joy, not only will we experience inner happiness and peace, but the fruits of our practice will swiftly arise.

Over to you...

● What sort of things bring joy into your life? What do you do to bring joy into your life and other people's lives?

Many Buddhas

Buddha is a title for anyone who is Enlightened. Siddattha became the first Buddha, and other people have become Buddhas since. Some Buddhists worship symbolic, imaginary Buddhas. The statues of symbolic Buddhas shown here are in Japan and Singapore.

Bringing joy into everyday life

The Buddha taught that there were four things that would bring about happiness in life: love, compassion, joy and equanimity.

● Love means wanting others to be happy.
● Compassion means showing love for people who are suffering.
● Joy means being happy at someones else's good fortune and not being jealous.
● Equanimity means keeping a calm and peaceful mind, no matter what happens.

Celebrating a commitment

A Buddhist marriage is a **commitment** between two people to live by the Buddha's teachings in their relationship. The Buddha said that the partners should be equals and respect each other.

A Buddhist bride in Cambodia. A monk has placed a white thread over her ear as a symbol of her commitment.

A Buddhist wedding

Buddhists celebrate a wedding in different ways, according to the customs of the country in which they live. In the UK, Buddhists may have a blessing after a legal ceremony at a register office. Buddhist weddings can take place in a temple or in another place, such as someone's home or a hotel. Family and friends of the couple are at the ceremony as well as people from the Buddhist community.

Commitment to the Buddha

Commitment ceremonies between two people vary from one Buddhist tradition to another. Sometimes Buddhist couples make up their own ceremony. The couple might recite the Five Ethical Precepts or some special verses. They might give each other rings and they might pass thread around to all their friends and family to show that they are all one community, just as they do in the naming ceremony.

The greatest happiness a human can imagine is the bond of marriage that ties together two loving hearts.

Carrie is 22. She describes her friend's wedding in Cambodia.

Last Sunday I went to my friend Chantavy's wedding in Cambodia. She was dressed in a bright blue dress. She wore gold jewellery and heavy makeup. The groom, Amara, wore a suit that he'd borrowed from a friend. The wedding was outdoors, under a square, red umbrella. The ceremony was short and there was a party afterwards with lots of food — oily rice with vegetables. The music was very loud! They played Cambodian pop songs as well as some Western ones.

A couple in Cambodia get covered with party string and foam.

Over to you...

● Have you ever been to a wedding? How did it compare with this Buddhist wedding?

Death, rebirth and Nibbana

Buddhists believe that death is a natural part of the cycle of life. Buddhism teaches that the body wears out and dies, but our awareness travels on, through one new life to another, ever changing.

The lotus flower grows in ponds, beginning in muddy darkness and growing towards the sun. In Buddhism, it symbolises the way humans can choose to move towards Enlightenment.

The cycle of life

In each life we change. We might behave more kindly or less kindly, or become more aware of how we affect other people. Buddhists believe that the way we behave today will affect us tomorrow and in our next life. We always have a choice between acting kindly or selfishly.

The cycle of life from birth to death to rebirth ends only when we stop wanting things that cannot bring us real happiness. This is known as Enlightenment. It is also called **Nibbana**, when the 'fires' of greed and hatred have been 'blown out'. After this, a person is not reborn but reaches a calm state called **Parinibbana**.

The unanswerable question

The Buddha reached Enlightenment when he was about 30 years old. He died at the age of 80, after a long life of teaching others the way. Before he died, his followers asked him what would happen to him after he died.

The Buddha said the question could not be answered. It was a mystery, impossible to explain in words. He said it was not important. The only thing that mattered was to understand what causes suffering and how to move towards happiness. His last words were: "With mindfulness, keep doing your best!"

Some Buddhists show the cycle of rebirth with the Wheel of Life, like this one. It shows how actions have consequences and how one life leads to another.

A monk worshipping in front of a statue of the Buddha in Kusinara, India, where the Buddha died.

A garland of flowers has been placed by the Buddha's head as a decoration and offering.

Celebrating the end of a life

Buddhist funerals vary around the world. The most important thing is to celebrate the life that has ended and help the person move peacefully towards a new life.

A Buddhist funeral in Thailand

For six evenings after a person has died, monks go to their home to pray. Flowers and photographs of the person are put on the coffin. After a week, a **cremation** takes place at the temple. The body is burnt until it turns into ashes. Guests wear dark clothes with white shirts, and bring gifts or money for the family. Then food is offered to the guests and everyone has a good chat. People may be sad, but they also know that everything must come to an end.

A celebration of life

The Buddha taught that nothing lasts for ever and everything changes, including us. Happiness lies in living kindly, loving people and things, while remembering that eventually everything has to end. Death is part of a natual process – the cycle of life and death and rebirth.

Charini is 30 years old. She lives in America. Her uncle has just died.

When Uncle Pururavas died, I was very sad, even though I knew he would be reborn into a better life. I felt sad because I would miss him. At his **memorial service**, the altar was decorated with flowers, fruit, food and drink. The scents were rich and powerful and I felt that Uncle Pururavas would enjoy this. We prayed and chanted and I told some of Uncle Pururavas's favourite jokes and read out his favourite Buddhist saying: "He is able who thinks he is able."

Over to you...

● Have you ever been to a funeral or memorial service? How did it celebrate the life of the person who had died?

● What do you believe happens after death?

Blessings printed on the prayer flags are released on the wind for the benefit of all beings.

Prayer flags flutter over a memorial to climbers who died on Mount Everest in Nepal.

Buddhists escort a dead body in a funeral procession in Burma.

Glossary and more information

Buddha The founder of Buddhism. Also, any *Enlightened* person.

Buddhist Someone who follows the religion founded by Siddattha Gotama. Also, a word that describes things belonging to Buddhism.

commitment A promise to do something.

community A group of people in, for example, a town, or school or the world.

cremation The burning of a dead body, until it turns to ashes.

Dhamma The teachings of the *Buddha*, which tell us how to reach *Enlightenment*.

Enlightenment The goal of Buddhism – the perfection of *wisdom* and kindness.

faith A strong belief.

generosity The act of freely sharing what we have with other people.

incense Something that is burnt to make a room smell special. Some *Buddhists* burn it during *meditation* to help them feel calm.

kamma The *Buddha*'s teaching that all of our actions have consequences.

meditation A *Buddhist* practice of being still and relaxed, calming the mind and body and concentrating deeply.

memorial service A service to honour and remember a person who has died.

Nibbana The state of perfect peace when the 'fires' of greed, hatred and ignorance have been 'blown out'.

novice Someone who is new to life in a monastery or nunnery.

Parinibbana When a *Buddha* dies, ending his or her cycle of births and deaths.

philosophy A way of thinking about life.

rebirth The *Buddhist* teaching that when a person dies, they pass on to a new human life.

relationship The way in which two or more people are connected with each other.

ritual A ceremony in which a series of actions are performed in a set order.

scriptures The sacred writings of a religion.

shrine A place people go to, to remember and show respect for someone they admire.

temple A place of worship.

tradition A custom, or a particular way of doing things, within one religion.

vinaya The rules or way of life that *Buddhist* monks and nuns follow in a monastery.

Wesak A festival celebrating the *Buddha*'s *Enlightenment* and often also his birthday.

wisdom In Buddhism, understanding the Way Life Really Is, as the *Buddha* did.

Things to do

Ask your teacher to help you to organise a visit to a Buddhist temple. There are hundreds in the UK. Look on the internet to find one near you. Always contact a temple before you go, to ask if you can visit with a group.

The Buddha said that anyone could become Enlightened, like him. Discuss with some friends what this means. Make a list of all the things the Buddha said about behaviour that brings happiness and leads to Enlightenment.

Tell the story of the Buddha to some younger children. You could tell the story with puppets or drawings. Or ask your teacher to help you make a PowerPoint presentation to your class.

Find out why the symbol of the lotus flower is so important to the Buddhist religion.

More information

Find out more about Buddhism on these websites or from the Buddhist organisations and monasteries listed below.

Websites

www.clear-vision.org
The Clear Vision Trust makes teaching materials for Buddhism. On the website there are stories about Buddhism and some games and quizzes. You can also watch videos of some Buddhists answering questions about themselves and their religion.
www.bbc.co.uk/schools/religion/buddhism
A page from the BBC schools website, with a short introduction to Buddhism.

Organisations and monasteries

The Clear Vision Trust
16–20 Turner Street, Manchester, M4 1DZ

Amaravati Buddhist Monastery
St. Margaret's Lane, Great Gaddesden, Hemel Hempstead, Hertfordshire, HP1 3BZ
www.amaravati.org/abmnew/index.php

Kagyu Samye Ling Monastery and Tibetan Centre
Eskdalemuir, Langholm, Dumfriesshire, DG13 0QL
www.samyeling.org

London Buddhist Centre
51 Roman Road, Bethnal Green, London, E2 0HU
www.lbc.org.uk

Manchester Buddhist Centre
16–20 Turner Street, Manchester, M4 1DZ
www.manchesterbuddhistcentre.org.uk

Index

AB
actions 13, 14, 16, 18, 26, 27
animals 12, 19
babies 6–7
beliefs 12, 13, 14, 15, 16, 22, 26
birth 6–7, 26
the Buddha's 8
blessings 6, 20, 24, 29
brides 24
Buddha, the 8–9, 10–11, 12–13, 14, 16, 18, 19, 20, 21, 23, 24, 26, 27, 28
birthday 9
teachings 8, 10, 12–13, 18, 20, 23, 24, 27, 28
Buddhas 6, 8, 14, 22–23
Laughing 22
of compassion 7
Burma 10, 11, 14, 29

C
Cambodia 21, 24, 25
candles 9, 20
celebrations 6, 9, 24, 28
ceremonies 6, 7, 24
naming 6, 7, 24
wedding 24–25
chanting 6, 20, 28
China 22
coffins 28

communities 6, 9, 10–11, 20, 24
compassion 23
contentment 14, 22
cremations 28
cycle of life 26–27

DE
Dalai Lama 15
death 8, 26–29
the Buddha's 26, 27
Dhamma 12, 13
Dhammachakka (see Wheel of Dhamma)
Eightfold Path 12, 13
Enlightenment 13, 22, 23, 26
the Buddha's 8–9, 26
environment 19
equanimity 23
Everest, Mount 29

FG
fair trade 16, 19
families 6, 10, 11, 20, 24, 28
the Buddha's 8
feasts 9
festivals 9, 11, 18, 20
Wesak 9, 18
Five Ethical Precepts 18, 24
flowers 6, 19, 20, 27, 28
food 10, 11, 16, 19, 25, 28

food miles 19
Four Noble Truths 12
friends 9, 10, 20, 24, 25
friendship 11
fruit 20, 28
funerals 28–29
funeral processions 29
generosity 14, 16, 18, 22
gifts 11, 28
grooms 25

HIJK
halos 8
happiness 8, 12, 14, 16, 18, 22, 23, 24, 26, 28
incense 20
India 27
Japan 23
joy 22–23
kamma 16
kindness 12, 13–14, 15, 16, 18, 22, 26, 28
Kusinara, India 27

LM
languages 20
Laughing Buddha 22
lay people 10
leaders 12, 15
Lhasa, Tibet 13
London 18
lotus flowers 6, 19, 26

love 18, 23, 24
marriage 24–25
meditation 8, 9, 10, 11, 20
memorials 29
memorial services 28
monasteries 10, 11, 13, 17
monks 6, 10, 11, 12, 14, 17, 20, 22, 24, 27, 28

NOPQ
names 6, 7
the Buddha's 8
naming ceremony 6, 7, 24
Nepal 9, 29
Newari people 9
Nibbana 26
novices 11
nuns 10, 20
offerings 19, 27
Pali 20
Parinibbana 26
peace 11, 14, 23
prayers 15, 28
prayer flags 29
prayer wheels 20

R
rebirth 15, 26, 27, 28
register office 24
relationships 18, 24
rings, wedding 24
rituals 6
robes 11, 17

S
Sanskrit 20
scriptures 6, 20
shrine hall 20
Siddattha (see Buddha, the)
Singapore 23
Sri Lanka 9
statues 22, 23, 27
suffering 8, 12, 13, 16, 23, 26
symbols 24, 26

TUV
temples 6, 9, 11, 15, 19, 20, 21, 24, 28
Thailand 9, 28
threads 6, 9, 24
Tibet 13, 15
traditions 20, 24
UK 6, 7, 11, 17, 18, 24
vegetarians 19
Vietnam 9
vinaya 11

WXYZ
Way Life Really Is 8, 12
Way of life 8–23
weddings 24–25
Wesak 9, 18
Wheel of Dhamma 13
Wheel of Life 27
wisdom 22
worship 20–21, 23, 27

Picture credits

The publisher would like to thank the following for their kind permission to reproduce their photographs:

Position key: c=centre; b=bottom; t=top; l=left; r=right

1c: iStockphoto; 3br: Claire Stour/World Religions Photo Library; 3tr: Alex Masi/World Religions Photo Library; 3bc: Julian Worker/World Religions Photo Library; 4bl: Raisa Kanareva/shutterstock; 6cl: Chinch Gryniewicz/World Religions Photo Library; 7bc: iStockphoto; 7tl: Glenda M Powers/shutterstock; 8cl: Christine Osborne/World Religions Photo Library; 9c:

Nick Dawson/World Religions Photo Library; 10cl: Christine Osborne/World Religions Photo Library; 11bc: Chinch Gryniewicz/World Religions Photo Library; 11tr: Christine Osborne/World Religions Photo Library; 12bl: Christine Osborne/World Religions Photo Library; 13cr: Nick Dawson/World Religions Photo Library; 14bc: Christine Osborne/World Religions Photo Library; 15tc: Nick Dawson/World Religions Photo Library ; 16cl: Cole Vineyard/iStockphoto; 16c: Monkey Business Images/shutterstock; 17c: Chinch Gryniewicz/World Religions Photo Library; 18bc: Chinch gryniewicz/World Religions Photo Library; 19tc: Christine Osborne/World Religions Photo Library; 20bl: Raisa Kanareva/shutterstock; 20cl: szefei/shutterstock;

21c: Claire Stout/World Religions Photo Library; 22bc: weiyee/shutterstock; 23cr: Frank van deh Bergh/istockphoto; 23cl: Jeremy Edwards/iStockphoto Hoare/World Religions Photo Library; 24cl: Claire Stout/World Religions Photo Library; 25tl: Darren Hubley/istockphoto; 25c: Claire Stout/World Religions Photo Library; 26cl: Bortal Pavel/shutterstock; 26tl: Alex James Bramwell/shutterstock; 27tl: Chinch Gryniewicz/World Religions Photo Library; 27bc: Nick Dawson/World Religions Photo Library; 28bl: VikramRaghuvanshi/iStockphoto; 29c: Jason Maehl/shutterstock; 29bl: Christine Osborne/World Religions Photo Library

Cover photograph © dbimages/Alamy